ISBN   978-0-544-25011-6

1 2 3 4 5 6 7 8 9 10   XXXX   24 23 22 21 20 19 18 17 16 15
4500000000                        B C D E F G

# Table of Contents

# Introduction

Extra practice is often the key to better accuracy and speed when working math problems. Learners can build confidence and ability as they review the skills necessary to understand a math concept and then apply those skills in a series of practice exercises. The **Head for Home Math** series provides additional practice with math skills.

*Head for Home: Division, Book 1,* is designed to reinforce math skills in division and provide additional practice to help learners improve their understanding of math concepts. This workbook covers key Division skills as outlined in the Common Core State Standards for Mathematics* for grades 3–4. Each lesson includes the following:

- An introduction explains the skill in student-friendly language and provides example problems with clear, step-by-step instructions.

- Multiple-choice and open-ended items allow students multiple opportunities to practice the skill.

By choosing this workbook, you are helping your child strengthen his or her understanding of math concepts and achieve continued success in math. Thank you for being involved in your child's learning. Here are a few suggestions for helping your child with math concepts.

- Read the instructions for each skill with your child and discuss the concepts.

- Practice math skills while riding in the car, shopping, or preparing meals. Help your child discover that math applies to everyday life.

- Check the lesson when it is complete. Note areas of improvement and praise your child for success. Also note areas of concern and provide additional support as necessary.

* The Common Core State Standards for Mathematics can be accessed at http://www.corestandards.org/Math.

# Skill Focus: Interpret Quotients of Whole Numbers

**Objective:** Interpret whole-number quotients of whole numbers.

Use **division** when you want to separate objects into groups of equal size. You can use division to find out how many are in each group or how many equal groups there are. The answer to a division problem is called the **quotient**.

**Example:** You have 12 marbles. You want to make 3 groups of equal size.
You put 4 marbles in each group.

**Say:** 12 divided by 3 equals 4.

**Write:** $12 \div 3 = 4$

The quotient when 12 is divided by 3 is 4. The quotient in this case represents the number of marbles in each group.

## Putting Counters in Equal Groups

**Example:** Emilia has 24 stickers to divide equally among each of 6 friends. How many stickers does she give to each friend?

**Step 1:** The number in each group is unknown, so divide.

**Step 2:** Place 1 counter at a time in each group until all 24 counters are used.

**Step 3:** There are 4 counters in each of 6 groups.

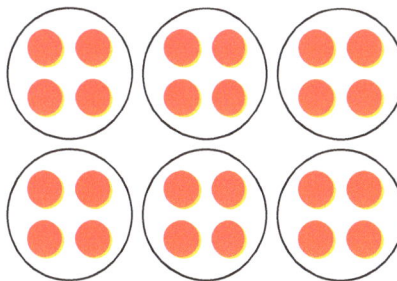

Use division to determine the number of groups of equal size.

**Example:** Bill is handing out 20 pens. He places 4 on each table. On how many tables can he place pens?

**Step 1:** What is the total number of pens?

There are ___20___ pens.

**Step 2:** What is the number in each group?

There are ___4___ in each group.

**Step 3:** What is the number of groups?
Use counters to find the number of groups.

There are ___5___ groups.

So, Bill can place pens on 5 tables.

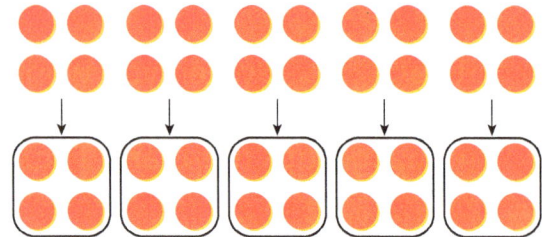

**Example:** Eva has 24 beads to make bracelets. Each bracelet will have 8 beads. How many bracelets will she make?

**Step 1:** What is the total number of beads?

There are ___24___ beads.

**Step 2:** What is the number in each group?

There are ___8___ in each group.

**Step 3:** What is the number of groups?
Draw beads to find the number of groups.

There are ___3___ groups.

So, Eva will make 3 bracelets.

# Interpreting Quotients of Whole Numbers

**Directions:** **Read each problem carefully. For the multiple-choice items, circle the letter of the correct answer. For the open-ended items, write or draw your answer in the space provided.**

**1** Janie has 15 dolls. She wants to give her 3 cousins the same number of dolls each. How many dolls will each of her cousins get?

**A.** 4

**B.** 5

**C.** 6

**2** Alicia has 12 eggs that she will use to make 4 different cookie recipes. If each recipe calls for the same number of eggs, how many eggs will she use in each recipe?

**A.** 2

**B.** 3

**C.** 4

**3** Brett picked 27 flowers from the garden. He plans to give an equal number of flowers to each of 3 people. How many flowers will each person get?

**4** Luis has 36 baseball cards. He puts 9 cards on each page in his album. How many pages does Luis fill?

A. 4

B. 6

C. 8

**5** Mr. Holden has 32 quarters in stacks of 4 on his desk. How many stacks of quarters are on his desk?

A. 4

B. 8

C. 16

**6** In his bookstore, Toby places 21 books on shelves, with 7 books on each shelf. How many shelves does Toby use?

**7** Write a division equation to represent the model below.

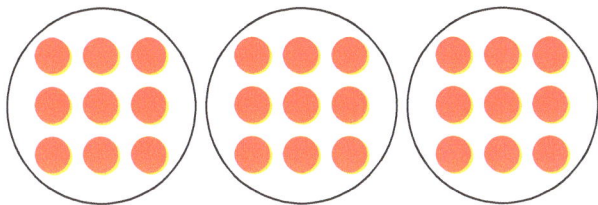

**8** Write a division equation to represent the model below.

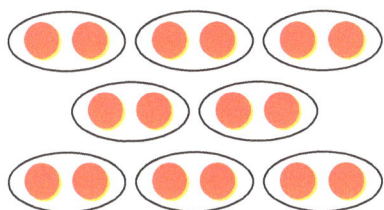

**9** Tanner has 30 stickers. He puts 6 stickers on each of 5 pages. Write a division equation to represent the situation.

**10** Jalyn collects 24 stones. She puts them in 4 equal piles of 6 stones each. Write a division equation to represent the situation.

# Skill Focus: Model Two-Digit by One-Digit Division

**Objective:** Fluently divide within 100 using models.

You can use a number line to divide. Make equal-sized jumps back to show an equal group.

## Dividing on a Number Line

**Example:** Mr. Carter has 15 baseball cards to split evenly among his three sons. How many cards does each of his sons receive? Divide 15 by 3.

**Step 1:** Look at the **dividend**. It shows the total number. Circle it on the number line.

**Think:** 15 cards to be divided

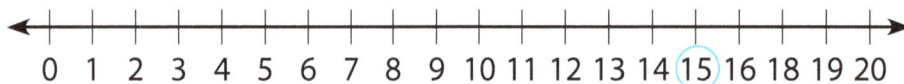

**Step 2:** Look at the **divisor**. It shows how many groups. Skip count back using that number.

**Think:** 3 sons

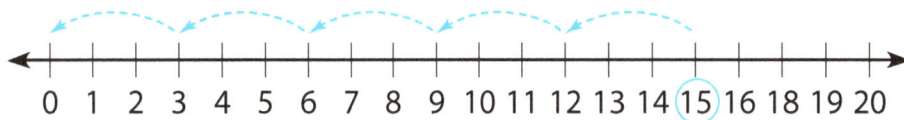

**Step 3:** Count how many jumps. Write the quotient.

**Think:** 5 in each group

$15 \div 3 = \underline{\quad 5 \quad}$

You can use pictures to divide.

**Example:** $15 \div 3$

**Step 1:** Look at the divisor. It shows how many in each group. Draw circles to show that many.

**Step 2:** Count how many circles. Write the quotient.

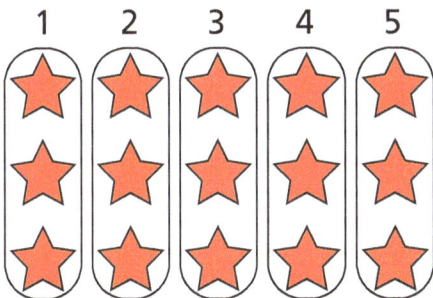

$15 \div 3 = \underline{\phantom{00}5\phantom{00}}$

**Directions:** Read each problem carefully. Write or draw your answer in the space provided.

**1** 18 ÷ 2 = _____

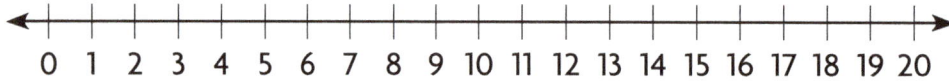

**2** 12 ÷ 6 = _____

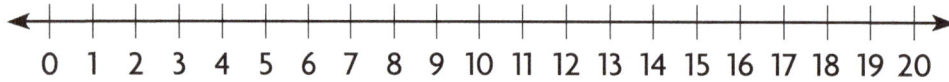

**3** 10 ÷ 2 = _____

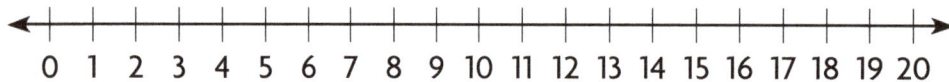

**4** 16 ÷ 4 = _____

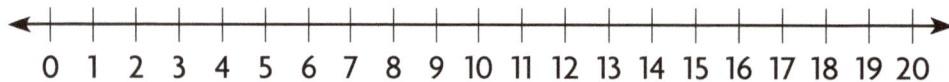

**5** 12 ÷ 4 = _____

**6** 10 ÷ 5 = _____

**7** 21 ÷ 3 = _____

**8** A jewelry store has 18 rings. The clerk will put 9 rings in each display box. How many boxes will the clerk need?

**9** Jacob buys 4 boxes of baseballs. Each box has the same number of baseballs. The total number of baseballs in the boxes is 36. How many baseballs are in each box?

**10** Renae's mother buys 48 bottles of water for her party. The bottles are in 8 equal groups. How many bottles are in each group?

# Skill Focus: Relate Multiplication and Division

**Objective:** Easily multiply and divide within 100 using the relationship between multiplication and division.

Multiplication and division are related. Division is the **inverse**, or opposite, operation of multiplication.

**Related facts** are a set of related multiplication and division equations.

## Using Models

You can use pictures to model related facts.

**Example:** There are 4 equal rows of apples.
There are 6 apples in each row.
There are 24 apples.

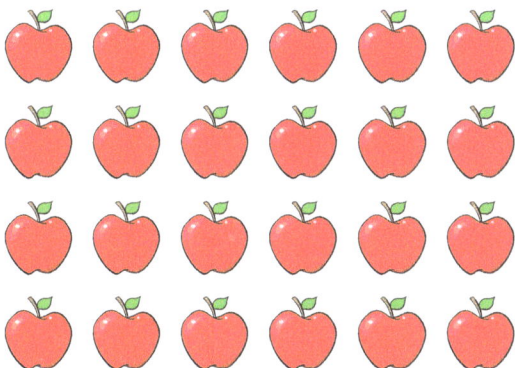

Write two multiplication equations and two division equations for the array.

factor × factor = product

$4 \times 6 = 24$
$6 \times 4 = 24$

dividend ÷ divisor = quotient

$24 \div 4 = 6$
$24 \div 6 = 4$

The equations show how the numbers 4, 6, and 24 are related.

The related facts are $4 \times 6 = 24$, $6 \times 4 = 24$, $24 \div 4 = 6$, and $24 \div 6 = 4$.

**Example:** $3 \times 7 =$ —————     $21 \div 7 =$ —————

**Step 1:** Draw circles around sets of 7 shapes. Think how many sets.

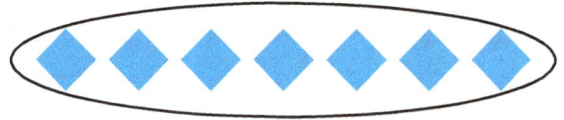

**Step 2:** Look at the multiplication sentence. Use the picture to solve it. Write the product.

$3 \times 7 =$ __21__

**Step 3:** Look at the division sentence. Use the picture to solve it. Write the quotient.

$21 \div 7 =$ __3__

## Using Mental Math

You can use mental math to divide. Think about multiplication facts to help you.

**Example:** Divide. $9\overline{)54}$

**Step 1:** Think of the division problem as a multiplication fact.

**Think:** $9 \times$ _____ $= 54$

**Step 2:** Think of the missing factor.

**Step 3:** The missing factor is the quotient of the division problem. Write the quotient.

$$9\overline{)54}^{\,6}$$

So, $54 \div 9 =$ __6__ .

# Relating Division and Multiplication

**Directions: Read each problem carefully. Write or draw your answer in the space provided.**

**1**

$4 \times 2 =$ _____    $8 \div 2 =$ _____

**2**

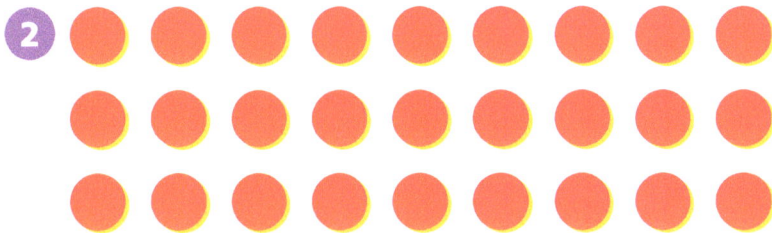

$9 \times 3 =$ _____    $27 \div 3 =$ _____

**3**

$4 \times 4 =$ _____    $16 \div 4 =$ _____

**4** 4 × _____ = 20, so 20 ÷ 4 = _____.

**5** 3 × _____ = 15, so 15 ÷ 3 = _____.

**6** 2 × _____ = 16, so 16 ÷ 2 = _____.

**7** 3 × _____ = 21, so 21 ÷ 3 = _____.

**8** 6 × _____ = 18, so 18 ÷ 6 = _____.

**9** Carlos has 25 stickers. He gives all of his stickers to his 5 friends. All of his friends receive the same number of stickers. How many stickers does each friend receive?

**10** Jane is baking blueberry pies for the fair. Each pie takes 4 cups of blueberries. If Jane has 12 cups of blueberries, how many pies can she bake?

**11** Kevin and Shonae have 35 marbles. They want to set up games with all of the marbles. Each game needs 5 marbles. How many games will Kevin and Shonae have?

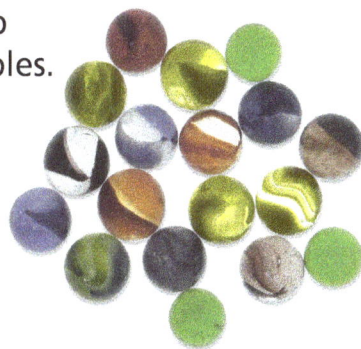

**12** Ming is giving 56 seashells to her cousins. She wants each cousin to get the same amount of seashells. If Ming has 8 cousins, how many shells will each cousin get?

# Skill Focus: Two-Digit by One-Digit Division

**Objective:** Fluently divide within 100, including finding the remainder.

A **division fact** is a number sentence in which the divisor and quotient are 9 or less. You should memorize these facts so that you are able to divide easily and quickly.

**Example:** Divide. Write the quotients as quickly as you can.

**Step 1:** Read the problem.

$7\overline{)42}$

**Step 2:** Quickly write the quotient.

$7\overline{)42}$ with quotient 6

**Step 3:** Check your answer. Multiply the quotient and the divisor. If you divided correctly, the product will be the same as the dividend.

6 × 7 = ___42___

**Step 4:** Repeat the steps to complete the problems below.

$3\overline{)24}$ = 8    $2\overline{)14}$ = 7    $8\overline{)64}$ = 8    $4\overline{)36}$ = 9

$5\overline{)15}$ = 3    $9\overline{)63}$ = 7    $6\overline{)48}$ = 8    $7\overline{)21}$ = 3

## Dividing with Remainders

In some division problems, a group will be left over that cannot be divided equally. This group is called the **remainder**.

**Example:** Divide. $7\overline{)45}$

**Step 1:** Think of the division problem as a multiplication fact.

**Think:** 7 × _____ = 45 or less

**Step 2:** Think of missing factors for which the products are close to the dividend. Be sure the products are not greater than the dividend.

**Think:** 7 × 6 = 42 (less than 45)
7 × 7 = 49 (greater than 45)

**Step 3:** Write the quotient. Multiply. Write the product under the dividend. Then subtract.

```
      6
  7)45
   -42  ◄── product
   ───
    3
```

**Step 4:** The difference is the remainder. Write the remainder next to the quotient. Use the letter **r** to show it is the remainder.

```
    6 r3
 7)45
  -42
  ───
   3
```

So, 45 ÷ 7 = ___6 r3___.

# Dividing Two-Digit Numbers
## by One-Digit Numbers

**Directions:** Read each problem carefully. Write or draw your answer in the space provided.

| | |
|---|---|
| **1** $6\overline{)24}$ | **2** $7\overline{)28}$ |
| **3** $7\overline{)49}$ | **4** $9\overline{)18}$ |
| **5** $8\overline{)56}$ | **6** $6\overline{)48}$ |
| **7** $4\overline{)32}$ | **8** $3\overline{)21}$ |
| **9** $8\overline{)40}$ | **10** $5\overline{)45}$ |
| **11** $2\overline{)16}$ | **12** $6\overline{)36}$ |

**13** $3\overline{)28}$

**14** $4\overline{)31}$

**15** $5\overline{)27}$

**16** $8\overline{)35}$

**17** $9\overline{)83}$

**18** $3\overline{)25}$

**19** $6\overline{)50}$

**20** $7\overline{)18}$

**21** $9\overline{)66}$

**22** $5\overline{)33}$

**23** Mrs. Sanchez bakes 25 muffins for a bake sale. She puts the muffins into packages of 4. How many muffins will Mrs. Sanchez have left?

**24** The animal shelter has 42 bags of dog food. The workers use 6 bags of food each day. How many days will the dog food last?

**25** Salima buys a 72-count package of paper. She divides the paper into 9 equal groups to make picture books. How many pieces of paper will be in each book?

**26** The Bear Factory is shipping out 86 toy bears. The factory packs 9 bears in a box. How many boxes will the factory need to ship all the bears?

# Skill Focus: Solve for an Unknown

**Objective:** Determine the unknown whole number in a division equation.

Models can help you find the unknown factor in a division equation.

## Using Base-Ten Blocks

**Example:** Andre got 3 hits in each of his baseball games. He has played 4 baseball games. How many hits has he had in all?

Find the unknown factor.   $3 = \blacksquare \div 4$

**Step 1:** Use cubes to model 4 groups of 3.

**Step 2:** Skip count by 3s four times to find how many in all.

3, 6, 9, 12

$\blacksquare$ = _____12_____

$3 =$ _____12_____ $\div 4$

So, Andre had _____12_____ hits in all.

You can also use square tiles to help you find the unknown factor in a division equation.

**Example:** Find the unknown factor.   $4 = \blacksquare \div 6$

You can use square tiles to find the unknown factor.

**Step 1:** Use tiles to model 4 rows of 6.

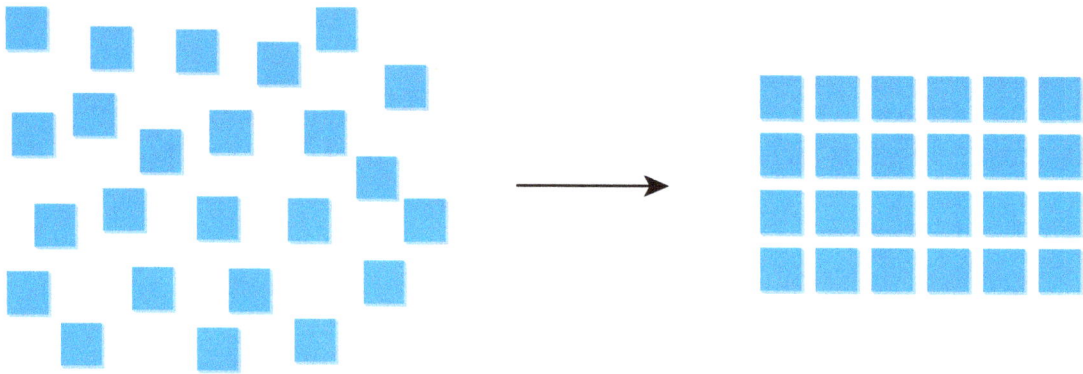

**Step 2:** Skip count by 6s four times to find how many in all.

6, 12, 18, 24

$\blacksquare = \underline{\phantom{xx}24\phantom{xx}}$

$4 = \underline{\phantom{xx}24\phantom{xx}} \div 6$

So, 4 rows of 6 equals $\underline{\phantom{xx}24\phantom{xx}}$.

# Solving for an Unknown

**Directions:** Read each problem carefully. For multiple-choice items, circle the letter of the correct answer. For the open-ended items, write or draw your answer in the space provided.

**1** Use square tiles to make an array. Solve.
How many rows of 7 are in 28?

**2** Use square tiles to make an array. Solve.
How many rows of 5 are in 15?

**3** Make an array to show 18 tiles in 3 rows.
Then write a division equation.

**4** Make an array to show 20 tiles in 4 rows.
Then write a division equation.

Solve for an Unknown
Head for Home: Division, Book 1    25

**5** $4 = \blacksquare \div 5$

$\blacksquare =$ _____

**6** $54 \div 6 = b$

$b =$ _____

**7** $16 \div p = 8$

$p =$ _____

**8** $10 \div \blacksquare = 5$

$\blacksquare =$ _____

**9** A dressmaker has 24 buttons. He needs 3 buttons to make one dress. How many dresses can he make with 24 buttons?

**A.** 6

**B.** 7

**C.** 8

**10** Liana buys 36 party favors for her 9 guests. She gives an equal number of favors to each guest. How many party favors does each guest get?

**A.** 4

**B.** 5

**C.** 6

**11** Mr. Reynolds, the gym teacher, divided a class of 16 students into 2 equal teams. How many students were on each team?

**A.** 32

**B.** 14

**C.** 8

**12** Sixty-four students are going on a field trip. There is 1 adult for every 8 students. How many adults are there?

**A.** 1

**B.** 8

**C.** 56

# Skill Focus: Division as Unknown Factors

**Objective:** Understand division as an unknown factor problem.

You can use a multiplication table to find unknown variables.

## Using a Multiplication Table

**Example:** Find the quotient of 30 ÷ 10.

Think of a related multiplication fact.

$10 \times \blacksquare = 30$

**Step 1:** Find the row for the factor, 10.

This number is the divisor.

**Step 2:** Look across the row to find the product, 30.

This number is the dividend.

| ✕ | 0 | 1 | 2 | 3 | 4 | 5 | 6 | 7 | 8 | 9 | 10 |
|---|---|---|---|---|---|---|---|---|---|---|----|
| 0 | 0 | 0 | 0 | 0 | 0 | 0 | 0 | 0 | 0 | 0 | 0 |
| 1 | 0 | 1 | 2 | 3 | 4 | 5 | 6 | 7 | 8 | 9 | 10 |
| 2 | 0 | 2 | 4 | 6 | 8 | 10 | 12 | 14 | 16 | 18 | 20 |
| 3 | 0 | 3 | 6 | 9 | 12 | 15 | 18 | 21 | 24 | 27 | 30 |
| 4 | 0 | 4 | 8 | 12 | 16 | 20 | 24 | 28 | 32 | 36 | 40 |
| 5 | 0 | 5 | 10 | 15 | 20 | 25 | 30 | 35 | 40 | 45 | 50 |
| 6 | 0 | 6 | 12 | 18 | 24 | 30 | 36 | 42 | 48 | 54 | 60 |
| 7 | 0 | 7 | 14 | 21 | 28 | 35 | 42 | 49 | 56 | 63 | 70 |
| 8 | 0 | 8 | 16 | 24 | 32 | 40 | 48 | 56 | 64 | 72 | 80 |
| 9 | 0 | 9 | 18 | 27 | 36 | 45 | 54 | 63 | 72 | 81 | 90 |
| 10 | 0 | 10 | 20 | 30 | 40 | 50 | 60 | 70 | 80 | 90 | 100 |

**Step 3:** Look up to the top row to find the unknown factor, ___3___.

This is the quotient.

Since 10 × 3 = 30, then 30 ÷ 10 = ___3___.

So, 30 ÷ 10 = ___3___.

**Example:** Find the quotient of 42 ÷ 6.

Think of a related multiplication fact.

$6 \times$ ▢ $= 42$

**Step 1:** Find the row for the factor, 6.

| × | 0 | 1 | 2 | 3 | 4 | 5 | 6 | 7 | 8 | 9 | 10 |
|---|---|---|---|---|---|---|---|---|---|---|---|
| 0 | 0 | 0 | 0 | 0 | 0 | 0 | 0 | 0 | 0 | 0 | 0 |
| 1 | 0 | 1 | 2 | 3 | 4 | 5 | 6 | 7 | 8 | 9 | 10 |
| 2 | 0 | 2 | 4 | 6 | 8 | 10 | 12 | 14 | 16 | 18 | 20 |
| 3 | 0 | 3 | 6 | 9 | 12 | 15 | 18 | 21 | 24 | 27 | 30 |
| 4 | 0 | 4 | 8 | 12 | 16 | 20 | 24 | 28 | 32 | 36 | 40 |
| 5 | 0 | 5 | 10 | 15 | 20 | 25 | 30 | 35 | 40 | 45 | 50 |
| 6 | 0 | 6 | 12 | 18 | 24 | 30 | 36 | 42 | 48 | 54 | 60 |
| 7 | 0 | 7 | 14 | 21 | 28 | 35 | 42 | 49 | 56 | 63 | 70 |
| 8 | 0 | 8 | 16 | 24 | 32 | 40 | 48 | 56 | 64 | 72 | 80 |
| 9 | 0 | 9 | 18 | 27 | 36 | 45 | 54 | 63 | 72 | 81 | 90 |
| 10 | 0 | 10 | 20 | 30 | 40 | 50 | 60 | 70 | 80 | 90 | 100 |

**Step 2:** Look right to find the product, 42.

**Step 3:** Look up to find the unknown factor, 7.

7 is the factor you multiply by 6 to get the product, ____42____.

So, $6 \times 7 =$ ____42____.

Use this related multiplication fact to find the quotient.

Since $6 \times 7 = 42$, then $42 \div 6 =$ ____7____.

So, $42 \div 6 =$ ____7____.

# Dividing to Find Unknown Factors

**Directions:** Read each problem carefully. For multiple-choice items, circle the letter of the correct answer. For the open-ended items, write or draw your answer in the space provided.

**1** $2 \times \underline{\hspace{1cm}} = 10$   $\underline{\hspace{1cm}} = 10 \div 2$

**2** $3 \times \underline{\hspace{1cm}} = 12$   $12 \div 3 = \underline{\hspace{1cm}}$

**3** $3 \times \underline{\hspace{1cm}} = 27$   $\underline{\hspace{1cm}} = 27 \div 3$

**4** $8 \times \underline{\hspace{1cm}} = 64$   $64 \div 8 = \underline{\hspace{1cm}}$

**5** $4 \times \underline{\hspace{1cm}} = 16$    $16 \div 4 = \underline{\hspace{1cm}}$

**6** $5 \times \underline{\hspace{1cm}} = 45$    $45 \div 5 = \underline{\hspace{1cm}}$

**7** $6 \times \underline{\hspace{1cm}} = 42$    $42 \div 6 = \underline{\hspace{1cm}}$

**8** $8 \times \underline{\hspace{1cm}} = 32$    $32 \div 8 = \underline{\hspace{1cm}}$

**9** Pens cost 10¢ each. How many pens can Brent buy with 90¢?

  **A.** 9

  **B.** 10

  **C.** 90

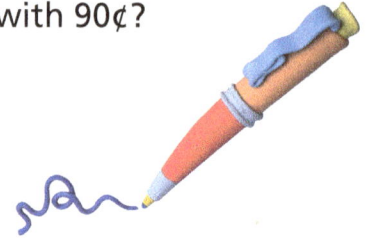

**10** Mrs. Marks wants to buy 80 pens. If the pens come in packs of 10, how many packs does she need to buy?

  **A.** 8

  **B.** 70

  **C.** 80

**11** Lucas has 36 pages of a book left to read. If he reads 6 pages a day, how many days will it take Lucas to finish the book?

  **A.** 8

  **B.** 7

  **C.** 6

**12** Juan has $24 to spend at the bookstore. If books cost $6 each, how many books can he buy?

  **A.** 30

  **B.** 18

  **C.** 4

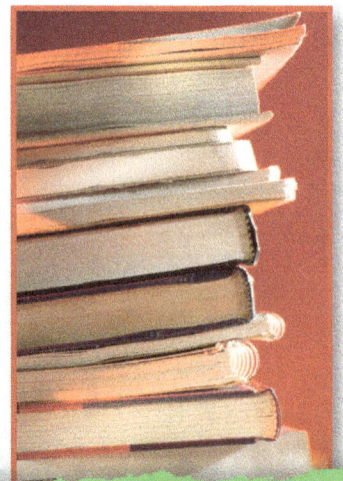

# Skill Focus: Estimation

**Objective:** Use mental computation and estimation strategies including rounding.

You can use multiples to estimate. A **multiple** of a number is the product of a number and a counting number.

## Estimating Quotients Using Multiples

**Example:** Find two numbers the quotient of 92 ÷ 4 is between. Then estimate the quotient.

**Step 1: Think:** What number multiplied by 4 is about 92?
Since 92 is greater than 10 × 4, or 40, use counting numbers 10, 20, 30, and so on to find multiples of 4.

**Step 2:** Multiply 4 by multiples of 10 and make a table.

| Counting Number | 10 | 20 | 30 | 40 |
|---|---|---|---|---|
| Multiple of 4 | 40 | 80 | 120 | 160 |

**Step 3:** Use the table to find the two multiples of 4 that are closest to 92.
20 × 4 = 80
30 × 4 = 120          ←——— 92 is between 80 and 120.

92 is closest to 80, so 92 ÷ 4 is about _____20_____.

## Using Rounding

You can estimate a quotient of a division problem by **rounding**. To round to the nearest ten, look at the ones digit. If the digit in the ones place is less than 5, round down. If the digit in the ones place is 5 or greater, round up.

**Example:** Find the quotient of 34 ÷ 5.

**Step 1:** Round the dividend to the nearest ten. Since 4 is less than 5, round down.

___30___ ÷ 5

**Step 2:** Divide. Write the estimated quotient.

30 ÷ 5 = 6

So, __6__ is an estimate quotient of 34 ÷ 5 when using rounded numbers.

## Using Compatible Numbers

You can estimate a quotient of a division problem by using a **compatible number**. Change the dividend to a number that can be easily divided by the divisor.

**Example:** Estimate the quotient. Use a compatible number. $3\overline{)87}$

**Step 1:** Change the dividend to a number that is easily divided by the divisor. Look for a division fact to help you.

87 ⟶ 90

**Step 2:** Divide. Write the estimated quotient.

$3\overline{)87}$ ⟶ $3\overline{)90}$

**Think:**
9 ÷ 3 = 3
90 ÷ 3 = ___30___

So, __30__ is an estimated quotient of $3\overline{)87}$ when using compatible numbers.

# Estimating Quotients

**Directions:** **Read each problem carefully. For multiple-choice items, circle the letter of the correct answer. For the open-ended items, write or draw your answer in the space provided.**

**1** Find two numbers the quotient of 95 ÷ 3 is between. Then estimate the quotient.

between _____ and _____

about _____

**2** Find two numbers the quotient of 75 ÷ 4 is between. Then estimate the quotient.

between _____ and _____

about _____

**3** Find two numbers the quotient of 53 ÷ 3 is between. Then estimate the quotient.

between _____ and _____

about _____

**4** Estimate $4\overline{)83}$. Use a compatible number.

   **A.** 2

   **B.** 20

   **C.** 30

**5** Estimate $2\overline{)58}$. Use a compatible number.

   **A.** 20

   **B.** 30

   **C.** 40

**6** Estimate $3\overline{)22}$. Use a compatible number.

   **A.** 7

   **B.** 10

   **C.** 20

**7** Estimate $3\overline{)59}$. Use a compatible number.

   **A.** 200

   **B.** 30

   **C.** 20

**8** A school cafeteria has 97 seats. The seats are divided equally into 5 sections. About how many seats are in each section?

**A.** 20

**B.** 30

**C.** 40

**9** Joy collects 86 aluminum cans in 4 hours. About how many cans does she collect per hour?

**A.** 10

**B.** 20

**C.** 30

**10** Angela and Trisha sell 85 cups of lemonade in 5 hours. About how many cups of lemonade do they sell each hour?

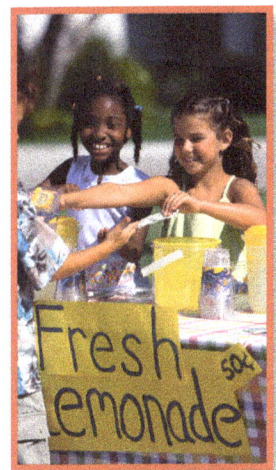

**A.** 20

**B.** 30

**C.** 40

# Skill Focus: One-Step Word Problems

**Objective:** Use division to solve one-step word problems.

A model or table can help you solve a word problem.

## Acting It Out

**Example:** There are 35 people going to the amusement park. They will all travel in 5 vans with the same number of people in each van. How many people will travel in each van?

**Step 1:** Start with 35 counters.

**Step 2:** Make 5 equal groups. Place 1 counter at a time in each group until all 35 counters are used.

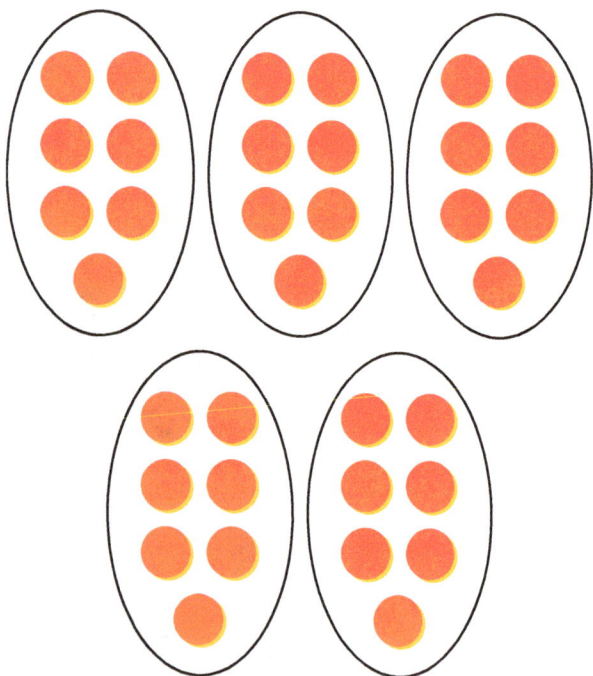

**Step 3:** Count the number of counters in each group.

So, __7__ people will travel in each van.

You can make a table to show all the possible ways something can be done. You can use the information in the table to solve problems.

**Example:** Cari has decorated 36 barrettes to sell at a craft fair. She needs to decide whether to put 4, 5, or 8 barrettes in each package with an equal number of barrettes in each package and with no barrettes left over. She made a table to find out how she might package the barrettes.

Complete the table to help you answer the word problem.

| Total Number of Barrettes | Number in Each Package | Division Sentence | Number of Packages | Number of Barrettes Left Over |
|---|---|---|---|---|
| 36 | 4 | $36 \div 9 = 4$ | 9 | 0 |
| 36 | 5 | $36 \div 5 = 7\ r1$ | 7 | 1 |
| 36 | 8 | $36 \div 8 = 4\ r4$ | 4 | 4 |

If Cari wants to have an equal number of barrettes in each package with none left over, she should put __4__ in each package.

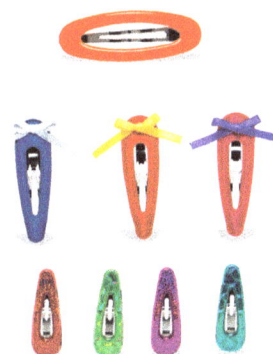

# Solving One-Step Word Problems

Directions: **Read each problem carefully and circle the correct answer.**

1. José packs 54 CDs into small boxes. Each box holds 9 CDs. How many boxes does José pack to hold all 54 CDs?

   A. 6

   B. 45

   C. 486

2. Mary volunteers at the library. She has 36 books to put on 4 empty shelves. If Mary puts an equal number of books on each shelf, how many books will be on each shelf?

   A. 7

   B. 8

   C. 9

3. Six customers at a toy store bought 18 jump ropes. Each customer bought the same number of jump ropes. How many jump ropes did each customer buy?

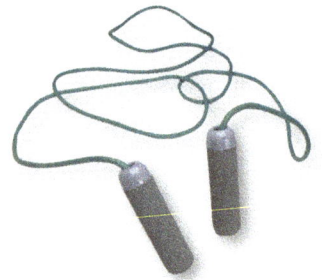

   A. 3

   B. 6

   C. 12

4. Hiro has 36 pictures of his summer trip. He wants to put them in an album. He wants to put the same number of pictures on each page and does not want any pictures left over. How many pages should Hiro use?

   A. 8

   B. 9

   C. 324

**5** Katia has 42 crayons. She buys a storage bin that has 6 sections. She puts the same number of crayons in each section. How many crayons does Katia put in each section of the storage bin?

A. 6

B. 7

C. 8

**6** Ms. Taylor's students give cards to each of the 3 class parent helpers. There are 24 cards. How many cards will each helper get if the students give an equal number of cards to each helper?

A. 6

B. 7

C. 8

**7** Jamie divides 20 baseball stickers equally among 5 of his friends. How many stickers does each friend get?

A. 4

B. 5

C. 15

**8** Maria needs 8 beads to make one bracelet. She has 72 beads. How many bracelets can Maria make?

A. 8

B. 9

C. 576

**9** Each case at a jewelry store holds 8 watches. How many cases are needed to hold 64 watches?

A. 8

B. 7

C. 6

**10** Antonio can put up to 6 clocks in a display case. He has 24 clocks. How many cases does he need?

A. 3

B. 4

C. 6

**11** Emma puts exactly 9 bracelets in a drawer. She has 45 bracelets. In how many drawers can Emma place the exact number of bracelets?

A. 4

B. 5

C. 6

**12** Mr. Chang tags each one of 40 pieces of jewelry. If there are 8 tags on a sheet, how many sheets of tags does he need?

A. 5

B. 6

C. 7

# Skill Focus: Two-Step Word Problems

**Objective:** Use division to solve two-step word problems.

You can use division and diagrams to solve word problems with two steps.

**Example:** Chloe bought 5 sets of books. Each set had the same number of books. She donated 9 books to her school. Now she has 26 books left. How many books were in each set that Chloe bought?

| Read the Problem | Solve the Problem |
|---|---|
| **What do I need to find?**<br><br>I need to find how many books were in each set. | **Step 1:** Begin with the number of books left. Add the number of books donated.<br><br>books left    books donated    $t$, total number of books<br><br>$26 + 9 = t$<br><br>$35 = t$ |
| **What information do I need to use?**<br><br>I need to use the information given:<br>Chloe bought 5 sets of books.<br>She donated 9 books.<br>She has 26 books left. | **Step 2:** Divide to find the number of books in each set.<br><br>$t$, total number of books    sets of books    $s$, books in each set<br><br>$35 \div 5 = s$<br><br>$7 = s$ |
| **How will I use the information?**<br><br>I will use the information to act out the problem. | So, __7__ books were in each set. |

## Drawing a Diagram

Use the strategy *draw a diagram* to solve a multi-step division problem.

**Example:** There are 72 third graders and 84 fourth graders going on a field trip. An equal number of students will ride on each of 4 buses. How many students will ride on each bus?

| Read the Problem | Solve the Problem |
|---|---|
| **What do I need to find?**<br><br>I need to find the number of students who will ride on each bus. | **Step 1:** Model the number of students in all using a bar diagram.<br><br><table><tr><td>72</td><td>84</td></tr></table><br>156 |
| **What information do I need to use?**<br><br>There are __72__ third graders and __84__ fourth graders. There will be __4__ buses. | **Step 2:** Model the number of buses and divide to find the number of students on each bus.<br><br><table><tr><td>39</td><td>39</td><td>39</td><td>39</td></tr></table><br>156 |
| **How will I use the information?**<br><br>I will make a bar diagram for each step. I will add _72 + 84_ to find the total number of students. I will divide by __4__ to find how many students will ride on each bus. | So, __39__ students will ride on each bus. |

# Solving Two-Step Word Problems

**Directions: Read each problem carefully. Circle the letter of the correct answer.**

**1** Joe has a collection of 35 DVD movies. He received 8 of them as gifts. Joe bought the rest of his movies over 3 years. If he bought the same number of movies each year, how many movies did Joe buy last year?

**A.** 24

**B.** 11

**C.** 9

**2** Tony had 4 equal sets of sports cards. He gave his friends 5 cards. Now he has 31 cards. How many cards were in each set?

**A.** 4

**B.** 9

**C.** 22

**3** Liz has a 24-inch-long ribbon. She cuts nine 2-inch pieces from her original ribbon. How many inches of the original ribbon are left?

**A.** 6

**B.** 12

**C.** 24

**4** Shelley buys 3 kites for $6 each. She gives the clerk $20. How much change should Shelley get?

**A.** $2

**B.** $11

**C.** $14

5. Sandy has 24 dolls. Then she gets 6 more dolls. She puts the dolls in boxes so that 6 dolls are in each box. How many boxes does Sandy use for her dolls?

A. 30

B. 6

C. 5

6. Dexter has $25 to spend on gifts for his friends. His mother gives him $5 more. If each gift costs $5, how many gifts can he buy?

A. 30

B. 5

C. 6

7. Miranda has 180 beads for making jewelry. She buys 240 more beads. She wants to store the beads in a case with 6 sections. She wants to put the same number of beads in each section. How many beads should Miranda put in each section?

A. 70

B. 40

C. 30

8. All 203 students at Polk School eat lunch at the same time. One day 19 students were absent. If 8 students sit at each table in the lunchroom, how many tables were used that day at lunch?

A. 184

B. 23

C. 11

**9** There are 3 trays of eggs. Each tray holds 30 eggs. How many people can be served if each person eats 2 eggs?

A. 15

B. 45

C. 90

**10** There are 8 pencils in a package. How many packages will be needed for 28 children if each child gets 4 pencils?

A. 9

B. 14

C. 56

**11** Misty has 84 photos from her vacation and 48 photos from a class outing. She wants to put all the photos in an album with 4 photos on each page. How many pages does she need?

A. 12

B. 21

C. 33

**12** There are 3 boxes of tangerines. Each box has 93 tangerines. The tangerines will be divided equally among 9 classrooms. How many tangerines will each classroom get?

A. 31

B. 27

C. 12

# Skill Focus: Model Three-Digit by One-Digit Division

**Objective:** Model dividing three-digit numbers by one-digit divisors.

You can use partial quotients and the Distributive Property to help you divide.

## Using Partial Quotients

Rectangular models can be used to record partial quotients.

**Example:** Divide 492 ÷ 4.

**Step 1:** Divide the hundreds place by 4.

400 ÷ 4 = 100

$$\begin{array}{r} 492 \\ -\ 400 \\ \hline 92 \end{array}$$

**Step 2:** Divide the tens place by 4.

90 ÷ 4 = 20 r10

$$\begin{array}{r} 92 \\ -\ 80 \\ \hline 12 \end{array}$$

**Step 3:** Divide the ones place by 4.

12 ÷ 4 = 3

$$\begin{array}{r} 12 \\ -\ 12 \\ \hline 0 \end{array}$$

__100__ + __20__ + __3__ = __123__

Use the Distributive Property and pictures to break apart numbers to make them easier to divide.

**Example:** Divide $128 \div 8$.

**Step 1:** Draw a picture to show 128.

**Step 2:** Think about how to break apart 128.
You know 8 tens $\div$ 8 = 10, so use 128 = 80 + 48.
Draw a quick picture to show 8 tens and 48 ones.

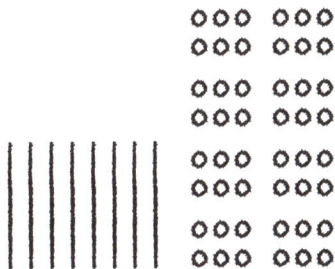

**Step 3:** Draw circles to show 8 tens $\div$ 8 and 48 ones $\div$ 8.
Your drawing shows the use of the Distributive Property.

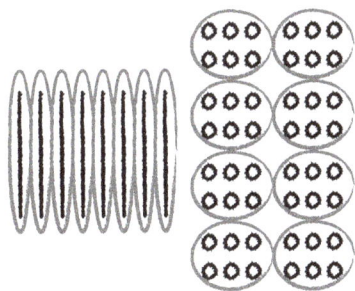

$128 \div 8 = (80 \div 8) + (48 \div 8)$

**Step 4:** Add the quotients to find $128 \div 8$.

$128 \div 8 = (80 \div 8) + (48 \div 8)$

$$= \underline{\quad 10 \quad} + \underline{\quad 6 \quad} = \underline{\quad 16 \quad}$$

**Directions:** Read each problem carefully. For multiple-choice items, circle the letter of the correct answer. For the open-ended items, write or draw your answer in the space provided.

**1** 8)184

**2** 6)258

**3** Divide 246 ÷ 3. Use a rectangular model to record the partial quotients.

**4** Divide 605 ÷ 5. Use a rectangular model to record the partial quotients.

**5** 492 ÷ 3 =

**6** 692 ÷ 4 =

**7** 232 ÷ 4 =

**8** 246 ÷ 6 =

**9** Jordan has 260 baseball cards. He divides them into 4 equal groups. How many cards are in each group?

    **A.** 40

    **B.** 65

    **C.** 1,040

**10** Cecily picks 219 apples. She divides the apples equally into 3 baskets. How many apples are in each basket?

    **A.** 73

    **B.** 75

    **C.** 657

**11** In Brett's town there are 128 basketball players on 8 different teams. Each team has an equal number of players. How many players are on each team?

A. 8

B. 16

C. 216

**12** The Wilsons drove 324 miles in 6 hours. If they drove the same number of miles each hour, how many miles did they drive in 1 hour?

A. 44

B. 54

C. 56

**13** Allison took 112 photos on vacation. She wants to put them in a photo album that holds 4 photos on each page. How many pages can she fill?

A. 48

B. 38

C. 28

**14** Hector saved $726 in 6 months. He saved the same amount each month. How much did Hector save each month?

A. $220

B. $121

C. $112

# Skill Focus: Three-Digit by One-Digit Division

**Objective:** Divide three-digit by one-digit numbers.

How do you know if your **trial quotient** is correct? If the remainder is more than the divisor, then your trial quotient is not enough. If you cannot subtract after multiplying the trial quotient and the divisor, then your trial quotient is too much.

```
       5   ← Not enough          7   ← Too much          6   ← Just right
   4)264                     4)276                    4)264
    −20                       −28                      −24
   ————                      ————                     ————
      6                                                  2
```

## Dividing by One-Digit Divisors

**Example:** Find 451 ÷ 4.

| **Step 1:** Begin at the left side of the dividend. Choose a trial quotient. Divide 4 by 4. Write 1 in the quotient. Multiply and subtract. Then bring down the next digit. | **Step 2:** 4 goes into 5 one time. Write 1 in the quotient. Multiply and subtract. Then bring down the last digit. | **Step 3:** Divide 11 by 4. Write 2 in the quotient. Multiply and subtract. The difference is the remainder. | **Step 4:** Check. Multiply the quotient by the divisor. Add the remainder. |
|---|---|---|---|

```
       1                   11                    112 r3                112
   4)451               4)451                  4)451                  ×   4
    − 4↓                 − 4↓                   − 4↓↓                 ————
   ————                 ————                   ————                   448
     05                   05                     05                  +   3
                         − 4↓                   − 4↓                 ————
                        ————                   ————                   451
                          11                     11
                                               − 08
                                               ————
                                                  3
```

## Dividing with Zeros in the Quotient

In some division problems, you must be careful to place a zero in the tens place or the ones place.

**Example:**

Divide the hundreds.

Multiply.

Subtract.

Compare.

Bring down.

$$\begin{array}{r} 1\phantom{00} \\ 4\overline{)429} \\ -4\phantom{0}\downarrow \\ \hline 02\phantom{0} \end{array}$$

There are not enough tens to divide. 2 < 4

Write 0.

Multiply.

Subtract.

Compare.

Bring down.

$$\begin{array}{r} 10\phantom{0} \\ 4\overline{)429} \\ -4\phantom{0} \\ \hline 02\phantom{0} \\ -0\downarrow \\ \hline 29 \end{array}$$

Divide the ones.

Multiply.

Subtract.

Compare.

Record the remainder.

$$\begin{array}{r} 107\ r1 \\ 4\overline{)429} \\ -4\phantom{00} \\ \hline 02\phantom{0} \\ -0\phantom{0} \\ \hline 29 \\ -28 \\ \hline 1 \end{array}$$

**Example:**

Divide the hundreds.

Multiply.

Subtract.

Compare.

Bring down.

$$\begin{array}{r} 2\phantom{00} \\ 3\overline{)721} \\ -6\phantom{0}\downarrow \\ \hline 12\phantom{0} \end{array}$$

Divide the tens.

Multiply.

Subtract.

Compare.

Bring down.

$$\begin{array}{r} 24\phantom{0} \\ 3\overline{)721} \\ -6\phantom{0} \\ \hline 12\phantom{0} \\ -12\downarrow \\ \hline 01 \end{array}$$

There are not enough ones to divide.
1 < 3 Write 0.

Multiply.

Subtract.

Compare.

Record the remainder.

$$\begin{array}{r} 240\ r1 \\ 3\overline{)721} \\ -6\phantom{00} \\ \hline 12\phantom{0} \\ -12\phantom{0} \\ \hline 01 \\ -0 \\ \hline 1 \end{array}$$

# Dividing Three-Digit by One-Digit Numbers

**Directions:** Read each problem carefully. For multiple-choice items, circle the letter of the correct answer. For the open-ended items, write or draw your answer in the space provided.

**1** 542 ÷ 5 =

**2** 724 ÷ 6 =

**3** 349 ÷ 9 =

**4** 794 ÷ 7 =

**5** 461 ÷ 3 =

**6** 315 ÷ 9 =

**7** 766 ÷ 2 =

**8** 604 ÷ 4 =

**9** Phil has 189 stamps to put into his stamp album. He puts the same number of stamps on each of 9 pages. How many stamps does Phil put on each page?

   **A.** 21

   **B.** 24

   **C.** 198

**10** There are 798 calories in six 10-ounce bottles of apple juice. How many calories are there in one 10-ounce bottle of apple juice?

   **A.** 123

   **B.** 133

   **C.** 79 r8

**Use the table for 11 and 12.**

| Rental Car Costs | |
|---|---|
| **Family** | **Total Cost** |
| Lee | $632 |
| Briggs | $985 |
| Santos | $328 |

**11** The Briggs family rented a car for 5 weeks. What was the cost of their rental car per week?

**12** The Lee family rented a car for 4 weeks. The Santos family rented a car for 2 weeks. Whose weekly rental cost was lower? Explain.

# Skill Focus: Review Division Facts

**Objective:** Know all quotients of two one-digit numbers.

If you know the multiplication facts, mastering the division facts should be easy.

## Using Counters

**Example:** You can use an array to solve 21 ÷ 3.

Use 21 counters. Make 3 equal rows.

There are __7__ in each row.

So, 21 ÷ 3 = 7.

The __21__ tells the total number of counters in the array.

The __3__ represents the number of equal rows.

The __7__ represents the number of counters in each row.

You can use a related multiplication fact to check your answer.

21 ÷ 3 = 7          3 × 7 = 21

So, 3 rows of 7 represents 21 ÷ 3 = 7 or 3 × 7 = 21.

# Dividing

**Directions:** Read each problem carefully. For multiple-choice items, circle the letter of the correct answer. For the open-ended items, write or draw your answer in the space provided.

| | | |
|---|---|---|
| **1** $4 \div 1 =$ | **2** $8 \div 4 =$ | **3** $9 \div 3 =$ |
| **4** $0 \div 5 =$ | **5** $10 \div 2 =$ | **6** $4 \div 4 =$ |
| **7** $6 \div 3 =$ | **8** $12 \div 4 =$ | **9** $15 \div 5 =$ |
| **10** $3\overline{)12}$ | **11** $5\overline{)25}$ | **12** $3\overline{)15}$ |
| **13** $4\overline{)20}$ | **14** $6\overline{)0}$ | **15** $4\overline{)16}$ |

**16** Complete the equation. $20 \div$ _____ $= 4$

A. 4
B. 5
C. 10

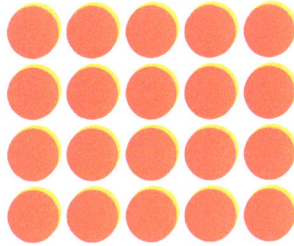

**17** Complete the equation. $24 \div$ _____ $= 6$

A. 4
B. 6
C. 12

**18** Complete the equation. $24 \div$ _____ $= 8$

A. 16
B. 4
C. 3

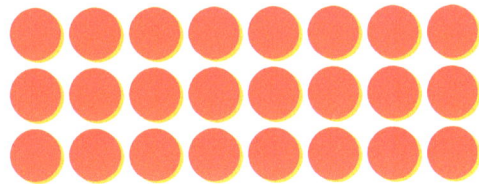

**19** Marla takes 8 socks out of the dryer. She puts the socks into pairs. How many pairs of socks does Marla have?

A. 2

B. 4

C. 16

**20** Mr. Martin buys 36 muffins for a class breakfast. He places them on plates for his students. If he places 9 muffins on each plate, how many plates does Mr. Martin use?

A. 4

B. 27

C. 45

**21** Ralph read 18 books during his summer vacation. He read the same number of books each month for 3 months. How many books did he read each month?

A. 21

B. 15

C. 6

**22** The art teacher has 48 paintbrushes. She puts 8 paintbrushes on each table in her classroom. How many tables are in her classroom?

A. 56

B. 7

C. 6

# Answer Key

## Interpret Quotients of Whole Numbers, pp. 3–7

3.OA.2

1. B
2. B
3. 9
4. A
5. B
6. 3
7. 27 ÷ 3 = 9 or 27 ÷ 9 = 3
8. 16 ÷ 8 = 2 or 16 ÷ 2 = 8
9. 30 ÷ 6 = 5 or 30 ÷ 5 = 6
10. 24 ÷ 4 = 6 or 24 ÷ 6 = 4

## Model Two-Digit by One-Digit Division, pp. 8–12

3.OA.7

1. 9
2. 2
3. 5
4. 4
5. 3
6. 2
7. 7
8. 2
9. 9
10. 6

## Relate Multiplication and Division, pp. 13–17

3.OA.7

1. 8; 4
2. 27; 9
3. 16; 4
4. 5, 5
5. 5, 5
6. 8, 8
7. 7, 7
8. 3, 3
9. 5 stickers
10. 3 pies
11. 7 games
12. 7 shells

## Two-Digit by One-Digit Division, pp. 18–22

3.OA.7

1. 4
2. 4
3. 7
4. 2
5. 7
6. 8
7. 8
8. 7
9. 5
10. 9
11. 8
12. 6
13. 9 r1
14. 7 r3
15. 5 r2
16. 4 r3
17. 9 r2
18. 8 r1
19. 8 r2
20. 2 r4
21. 7 r3
22. 6 r3
23. 1 muffin
24. 7 days
25. 8 pieces
26. 10 boxes

## Solve for an Unknown, pp. 23–27

3.OA.4

**1.** 4

**2.** 3

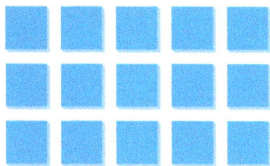

**3.** 18 ÷ 3 = 6 or 18 ÷ 6 = 3

**4.** 20 ÷ 4 = 5 or 20 ÷ 5 = 4

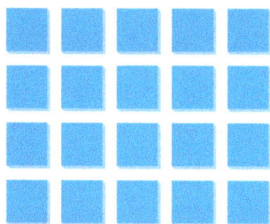

**5.** 20
**6.** 9
**7.** 2
**8.** 2
**9.** C
**10.** A
**11.** C
**12.** B

## Division as Unknown Factors, pp. 28–32

3.OA.6

**1.** 5, 5
**2.** 4, 4
**3.** 9, 9
**4.** 8, 8
**5.** 4, 4
**6.** 9, 9
**7.** 7, 7
**8.** 4, 4
**9.** A
**10.** A
**11.** C
**12.** C

## Estimation, pp. 33–37

3.OA.8

**1.** 30; 40; 30
**2.** 10; 20; 20
**3.** 10; 20; 20
**4.** B
**5.** B
**6.** A
**7.** C
**8.** A
**9.** B
**10.** A

## One-Step Word Problems, pp. 38–42

3.OA.3

**1.** A
**2.** C
**3.** A

4. B
5. B
6. C
7. A
8. B
9. A
10. B
11. B
12. A

## Two-Step Word Problems, pp. 43–47

3.OA.8

1. C
2. B
3. A
4. A
5. C
6. C
7. A
8. B
9. B
10. B
11. C
12. A

## Model Three-Digit by One-Digit Division, pp. 48–52

4.NBT.6

1. 23
2. 43

3. 82

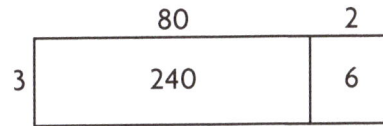

4. 121

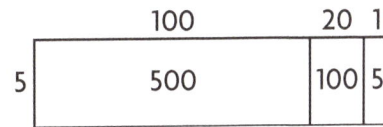

5. 164
6. 173
7. 58
8. 41
9. B
10. A
11. B
12. B
13. C
14. B

## Three-Digit by One-Digit Division, pp. 53–56

4.NBT.6

1. 108 r2
2. 120 r4
3. 38 r7
4. 113 r3
5. 153 r2
6. 35
7. 383
8. 151
9. A
10. B
11. $197
12. Lee family; possible explanation: Lee: $632 ÷ 4 = $158; Santos: $328 ÷ 2 = $164; $158 < $164

## Review Division Facts, pp. 57–60

3.OA.7

1. 4
2. 2
3. 3
4. 0
5. 5
6. 1
7. 2
8. 3
9. 3
10. 4
11. 5
12. 5
13. 5
14. 0
15. 4
16. B
17. A
18. C
19. B
20. A
21. C
22. C